The History of PC Gaming

21st Century Skills **INNOVATION LIBRARY**

Josh Gregory

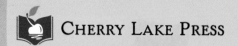
CHERRY LAKE PRESS

Published in the United States of America by Cherry Lake Publishing
Ann Arbor, Michigan
www.cherrylakepublishing.com

Reading Adviser: Beth Walker Gambro, MS, Ed., Reading Consultant, Yorkville, IL

Photo Credits: ©Pero Mihajlovic / Shutterstock, cover, 1; ©Gorodenkoff / Shutterstock, 5; ©Friends Stock / Shutterstock, 7; ©Everett Collection / Shutterstock, 9; ©Eleanor McDonie / Shutterstock, 13; ©Kjetil Kolbjornsrud / Shutterstock, 16; ©Randy Miramontez / Shutterstock, 20; ©Feng Yu / Shutterstock, 22; ©PeachLoveU / Shutterstock, 23; ©Casimiro PT / Shutterstock, 25; ©dean bertoncelj / Shutterstock, 26; ©Alberto Garcia Guillen / Shutterstock, 27; ©Phil's Mommy / Shutterstock, 29; ©UfaBizPhoto / Shutterstock, 31

Cherry Lake Press is an imprint of Cherry Lake Publishing Group.

Library of Congress Cataloging-in-Publication Data

Names: Gregory, Josh, author.
Title: The history of PC gaming / by Josh Gregory.
Other titles: History of personal computer gaming
Description: Ann Arbor, Michigan : Cherry Lake Publishing, 2022. | Series:
   Unofficial guides | Includes bibliographical references and index. |
   Audience: Grades 4-6 | Summary: "By building their own custom PCs, video
   game fans can tweak every detail to make sure they get the best possible
   experience every time they play. In this book, readers will explore the
   long, fascinating history of PC gaming, from the earliest innovations to
   the latest developments. Includes table of contents, author biography,
   sidebars, glossary, index, and informative backmatter"— Provided by
   publisher.
Identifiers: LCCN 2021042796 (print) | LCCN 2021042797 (ebook) | ISBN
   9781534199675 (library binding) | ISBN 9781668900819 (paperback) | ISBN
   9781668906576 (pdf) | ISBN 9781668902257 (ebook)
Subjects: LCSH: Computer games—History—Juvenile literature.
Classification: LCC GV1469.15 .G446 2022 (print) | LCC GV1469.15 (ebook)
   | DDC 794.809—dc23
LC record available at https://lccn.loc.gov/2021042796
LC ebook record available at https://lccn.loc.gov/2021042797

Cherry Lake Publishing Group would like to acknowledge the work of the Partnership for 21st Century Learning, a Network of Battelle for Kids. Please visit http://www.battelleforkids.org/networks/p21 for more information.

Printed in the United States of America
Corporate Graphics

Josh Gregory is the author of more than 125 books for kids. He has written about everything from animals to technology to history. A graduate of the University of Missouri–Columbia, he currently lives in Chicago, Illinois.

Contents

CHAPTER 1

Yesterday and Today

If you're into video games, you probably already know that there's nothing quite like playing on a high-end gaming PC. The latest PC **hardware** can run games more smoothly than any other video game system, and players can tweak settings to make games look and perform however they want.

PC gaming has always attracted an audience of serious technology enthusiasts. Many of these people are willing to spend a lot of time and money tweaking their setups to get the best possible gaming experience. For them, building and maintaining a PC is half the fun. But PC gaming isn't always about staying up to date with the latest and greatest. Many players have a great time playing even on outdated computers. They might play old games that don't require advanced hardware to run. Or they might check out the latest low-budget indie games, which are often just as fun as the biggest blockbuster releases but don't require such a powerful computer.

This kind of variety and flexibility has helped PC gaming remain in the spotlight for decades. Believe it or not, people have been playing PC games at home for more than 40 years. As countless consoles and other game systems have come and gone, the PC has remained a major player in the world of video gaming. Some of

A PC gaming setup is a big investment, but it can provide endless fun.

More Than a Gaming Machine

One reason PC gaming has stood the test of time is simply that many people need PCs for things other than gaming. Some people use them for work or school. Others have hobbies such as recording music or editing videos. Even if they aren't serious game players, these people might still want to pick up a game here and there. The Microsoft Windows operating system once came with free, built-in games such as Solitaire and Minesweeper. These simple games drew the attention of millions upon millions of people who would never even think about buying a video game console.

today's biggest games, including *Fortnite* and *Roblox*, got their start on the PC before they became available on other systems. Others, like *League of Legends* and *Valorant*, remain exclusive to PC players.

With such a long history, it should be no surprise that a lot of interesting things have happened since people first started playing PC games. And whether you're a PC veteran or a rookie player, you might be surprised to find out what things were like before your time. Are you ready to see how it all started?

Most professional gaming is done on powerful PCs.

CHAPTER 2

First Steps

The history of PC gaming dates back almost all the way to the invention of the first electronic computers. The first electronic, programmable computers were built in the 1940s. These massive machines often filled entire rooms. They were used solely by researchers, large companies, and the military. People did not keep them at home. And while these machines were amazing at the time, they were less powerful than even the weakest computers we use today. They were mainly used to do things like solve complex math problems and decode secret messages.

It didn't take long for people to start thinking up ways of using this new technology to have a good time. In the early 1950s, a team of British researchers built a computer capable of playing Nim, a game where two players take turns removing objects from several piles.

This computer, called Nimrod, was displayed as part of a public exhibit in 1951. Like other computers of the time, it was huge. People lined up for the chance to challenge the computer at a traditional game.

Ten years later, a team of computer scientists at the Massachusetts Institute of Technology unveiled a new kind of computer game called *Spacewar!*. Unlike anything that had come before, it displayed simple graphics of two spaceships on a computer screen. The ships were controlled by two different players, who attempted to defeat each other by firing

The massive computer known as ENIAC was built during World War II.

missiles. It was one of the first computer games to resemble the ones we play today.

Throughout the 1960s and 1970s, computer technology improved rapidly. The machines became smaller, more powerful, and less expensive. This allowed many more people to start using them and learning to write **code**. These computer enthusiasts could not simply download new games or buy them from stores like we do today. Instead, they often created their own games from scratch. They then shared the code for their homemade games with other PC hobbyists. Code might be published in magazines or simply traded between friends. Then other players would type all of the code back into their own computers, one line at a time. These early games typically had very simple graphics, or sometimes even no graphics at all, just text! The first gaming consoles and arcade machines were also created around this time, and video games started to become popular with the general public. But many PC fans remained dedicated to their hobby, even as it became easier to enjoy games in other ways.

The first personal computers were invented in the mid-1970s. This meant computer enthusiasts could finally have computers in their own homes. However, this wasn't as simple as it is today. The earliest PCs were very expensive, and there was no such thing as a pre-built machine. People had to purchase and assemble machines on their own, and that process was much more complex than it is today. Plus, they weren't able to go online and look up tips if they got stuck!

Playing in the MUD

Today, massively multiplayer online games, or MMOs, are a common and popular part of the video game landscape. But can you believe that players have been finding ways to adventure together online since the late 1970s? Long before the internet became a part of daily life, university students around the world created simple fantasy games that they could enjoy together by connecting through their schools' small online networks. These games were called multi-user dungeons, or MUDs.

Unlike the detailed fantasy worlds created using 3D graphics in today's MMOs, MUDs were text-based. Players typed in commands saying what they wanted their characters to do, and the game would tell them what happened. Meanwhile, they could talk to other players and work together to solve problems, just like in today's multiplayer games.

Believe it or not, some MUDs still exist today, and there are small but active communities around these games online. It's just one more example of the ways PC gaming has something to offer for just about everyone!

The end of the 1970s saw the creation of the first pre-built computers aimed at a mass audience. This allowed PCs, and PC gaming, to really take off throughout the 1980s. Companies like Apple and IBM offered machines that allowed anyone to take a computer home, plug it in, and get started. And as computers became more popular, it became much more common to see professionally created PC games on store shelves.

PC games of the 1980s tended to be very different from the ones available on game consoles such as the Nintendo Entertainment System or the Sega Master System. Console and arcade games tended to focus on fast-paced action. They had bright, colorful graphics and often required fast reflexes. The most popular PC games, on the other hand, tended to be much more complex, but slower paced.

Role-playing games (RPGs) like the *Ultima* series allowed players to get lost in detailed fantasy worlds. These games allowed players to explore however they chose, hold conversations with computer-controlled characters, and watch as a detailed story unfolded. Simulation games, such as the early versions of *Microsoft Flight Simulator*, gave players the chance to take to the skies in real-world aircraft. But instead of zooming around pulling off loop the loops, the games required players to fly carefully and pay attention to a variety of gauges and instruments, just like flying a real plane. Another popular PC game, *SimCity*, allowed players to build and oversee virtual cities, overseeing everything from tax laws to transportation systems. These kinds of games were very different from *Super Mario Bros.* or *Out Run*, and they often attracted a different kind of audience. As a result, while some people enjoyed games of all kinds, most stuck to either PC or console gaming.

PC games of the 1980s and 1990s typically came in large cardboard boxes, as many of them required a stack of disks to install and came with long, detailed instruction manuals.

CHAPTER 3

New Technology, New Games

In the 1990s, PC gaming moved on to a whole new level. With more powerful PC technology available, **developers** were able to create new kinds of games that were unlike anything seen before. One of the biggest new game genres to emerge on the PC in the 1990s was the first-person shooter, or FPS. Today, FPS games are extremely common. Almost anyone who plays video games is familiar with the concept of looking through the eyes of a game's main character as they move through a three-dimensional (3D) environment and attack enemies using a variety of weapons. But in the early 1990s, it was a major technical achievement to create these kinds of games. The style was popularized by 1992's *Wolfenstein 3D* and 1993's *Doom. Doom* was so popular that millions of people got into PC gaming just to give it a try.

The graphics in early FPS games were very impressive for the time. They moved quickly and smoothly, and they made players feel like they were truly inside of the game's world. However, it only took a couple of years for these early games to start looking out-of-date. The mid-1990s saw the release of the first video cards to focus on 3D graphics. Prior to this, developers had to build their games to run on the standard PC hardware used for other computer tasks. But as more and more PC gamers installed powerful video cards in their

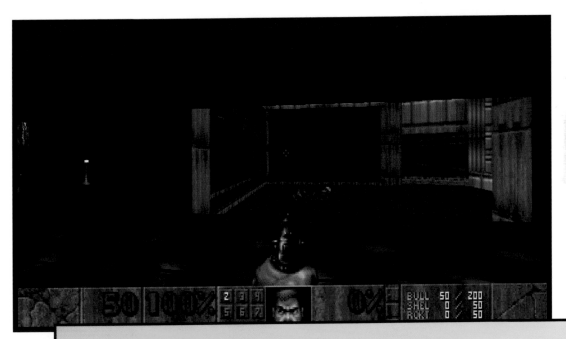

Doom's graphics wowed just about everyone when it was released, even if they weren't into video games.

machines, developers were able to push the limits of their games' graphics. And as the games got better-looking, video card manufacturers released even more powerful hardware.

This cycle of constant improvement in the graphics of PC games continues today. Just like new video game

Installing a new video card every few years (or even more often) has become common for serious PC gamers.

The latest FPS games have come a long way since *Wolfenstein 3D* and *Doom*.

consoles or smartphones always set off a frenzy of people looking for the hot new thing, the latest video cards tend to sell out as soon as they are released. And just as they have since the early 1990s, PC gamers often show off the power of their machines by playing the latest FPS games.

Many of the people who bought their first PCs in the 1990s were looking for a way to get online and try the internet for the first time. Before the 1990s, it wasn't possible to get internet access at home. It was used almost entirely by people at universities or in government organizations. But as the internet became more widely accessible, people started finding all kinds of ways to use it. One of them was, of course, gaming.

From Game Developers to Celebrities

One team of game developers, more than any other, was responsible for making FPS games the huge success they are today. Founded in 1991, id Software had success almost immediately with the release of *Wolfenstein 3D* and went on to even greater heights with the *Doom* and *Quake* series. By the middle of the decade, team members John Romero and John Carmack were among the most famous game developers in the world, with fans waiting breathlessly for their next creations.

The developers at id were known for their technical wizardry. With creative thinking and lots of programming know-how, they were able to make computers do things that no one had ever seen before. However, their games were more than just ways of showing off new technology. They were also a lot of fun to play! Decades later, many players still enjoy *Doom*, *Quake*, and other early id hits. With their carefully balanced gameplay and thoughtful level design, they are true classics that have stood the test of time.

Today, almost all video game systems can connect to the internet so players can join in the fun together online. But for a long time, the PC was the only place to be for online gaming. Sega's Dreamcast console let players go online starting in 2000, and the Xbox Live service was launched two years later. But PC gamers had already been competing online for years by that point. In fact, one of the things that made *Doom* such a popular game back in 1992 was its online multiplayer mode.

Because PCs were more or less the exclusive home of online gaming, many of the most popular games of the 1990s focused on head-to-head competition. However, they didn't sacrifice the depth and complexity that PC games had become famous for. Of course, FPS games only continued to grow in popularity. But many other kinds of games also helped set the PC apart as a unique way to play.

A new genre called the real-time strategy (RTS) game began drawing players in during the early 1990s. In games such as *Command and Conquer* and *Warcraft*, players gathered resources, built up home bases, and trained armies as they competed to conquer a map. Unlike earlier strategy games, players did not take turns or move slowly. They had

Today, tens of thousands of fans gather each year at the BlizzCon event to celebrate games like *StarCraft and World of Warcraft*, an MMORPG that follows in the footsteps of *Ultima Online and EverQuest*.

to think, plan, and act all at the same time. Careful strategizing and fast action were equally important, and players loved going online to compete against each other. By the end of the decade, RTS games like *StarCraft* were among the most popular on the planet, and the world's best players began competing in professional tournaments where lots of money was on the line. As a result, **esports** started moving into the mainstream.

Another style of online game to get its start on PCs was the massively multiplayer online role-playing game, or MMORPG. These games allowed huge numbers of players to adventure together in the same detailed fantasy world, all at once. One of the first MMORPGs to become popular was *Ultima Online*, released in 1997. *Ultima Online* was the latest game in the long-running *Ultima* series, and it carried on many of the things PC gamers had always loved about the series while offering a fresh online experience. Two years later, the MMORPG genre got even more popular with the launch of *EverQuest*. Millions of people created their own characters and went online to start exploring.

Getting online to play games and finding people to play with were not always as easy as they are today. For years, just about every game had its own system for connecting online. These systems could be clunky, slow, and difficult to use. Depending on the situation, players might find themselves spending more time finding a group of other players and connecting than actually playing. Internet connections were not as fast as they are today, and it was common to experience lag, or stuttering caused by a slow connection. But just like most aspects of PC gaming, players often found their own solutions for these issues. Some of

PCs of the 1990s were much heavier and bulkier than what you are probably used to today.

them **upgraded** their equipment and sought out the fastest-possible internet connections. Others built and operated **servers** for other players to connect to.

This spirit of do-it-yourself creativity is one of the key things that makes PC gaming unique. From the very beginning, PC enthusiasts often went so far as to develop their own games from scratch. When games like *Doom* and *Starcraft* became huge hits, many players found ways to keep the fun going by developing their own **mods**. Mods are unofficial additions and changes to commercially released games. Players create them and then share them with other players. In the days of *Doom*, modders passed around floppy disks containing homemade levels. Later, modders used the internet to trade files. Modding remains a big part of PC gaming today. Popular modders have found careers as professional game developers, and some mods have even gone on to become successful official releases.

Mod creators, or modders, often shared their games by copying files onto floppy disks like these and trading with friends.

CHAPTER 4

The Latest and Greatest

PC gaming is always changing. Something that seems state of the art one day could look like yesterday's news the next day. The most obvious example is graphics. All it takes is a quick glance to see how much better one game looks than another. But there are also other, less immediately noticeable ways that PC gaming has improved since it blew up in the 1990s.

One of the biggest changes has come in the way we discover and purchase new games. In the past, you would need to visit a store that sold games and sort through shelves of large boxes. Inside each game's box would be at least one floppy disk, CD, or DVD. And in some cases, there would be a whole pile of disks. Once you got your new game home, you had to use these disks to install it on your PC. Then, in most cases, you would need to put one of the disks in every time you wanted to play. Later, if the developers created a **patch** or other update for the game, you would need to manually download and install it.

That started to change as the internet got faster and more people set up connections in their homes. In 2003, the well-known game development studio Valve Software released a program called Steam. Steam allowed players to purchase digital

Today, buying the latest games is as simple as making a few clicks in Steam.

downloads of Valve's games. No disks were required. Players simply purchased a game, clicked a button to download it, and then Steam took care of the rest. Installations, patches, updates, and other tasks were all taken care of automatically. Many players signed up for the service right away so they could play Valve's latest game at the time, *Half-Life 2*. But that was only the

Before Steam, most PC games were released on DVDs. Today, many PC games are never released physically at all.

The Epic Games Store has gained a lot of users in recent years because it is the only way to play *Fortnite* on a PC.

beginning. Since then, Steam has completely changed the way PC gaming works. It started offering more convenient features, such as friend lists, chat windows, and built-in ways to tweak gameplay settings. Today, many PC gamers only purchase games through Steam.

Other digital storefronts, including the Epic Games Store and GOG Galaxy, have also become popular in recent years. Boxed, physical PC games, on the other hand, have become very rare. Many players don't even include disk drives when building their PCs.

Today, most of the biggest console games are also released for the PC. In many cases, PC players can even play online with console players. However, there are still certain kinds of games that are strongly associated with PCs. One of the most popular styles of PC games today is the multiplayer online battle arena, or MOBA. The earliest MOBAs were fan-made mods for

A Bright Future

Today, there are more ways to play video games than ever before. Aside from game consoles or gaming PCs, you can use smartphones, tablets, and other common household devices. But even with so many other options available, and with fewer people keeping desktop PCs at home for general use, PC gaming doesn't seem like it's going to be going away anytime soon. Over the past several years, sales for PC gaming hardware and accessories have seen a huge boom. Even with the release of new game consoles like the PlayStation 5 and Xbox Series X, many people still prefer to play on PCs.

It might be hard to believe, but *Minecraft* was once a small independent game that was released as a free download.

RTS games. Today, MOBAs like *Dota 2* and *League of Legends* are far more popular than any RTS game, and they can't be played anywhere but on a PC.

The PC is also home to more indie games than any other platform. Indie games are developed by small, independent teams instead of big companies. They tend to have simpler graphics than big-budget games, but that doesn't make them any less fun. For example, *Minecraft* started out as a little-known indie game that was only playable on PC. Since then, it has grown to be one of the most successful video games of all time!

As video games have gotten more and more popular, so have esports and streaming. And while it is possible to do those things on a video game console, the PC is by far the most widely used platform for both. Esports pros prefer to play on PCs because they can run games at a higher **frame rate** and use more precise controls. Streamers enjoy PCs for the same reasons, plus it gives them more control over their footage.

One of the biggest innovations in video games in recent years has been the introduction of affordable, high-end virtual reality (VR) units. It should come as no surprise that the PC is the preferred system for most VR enthusiasts. It takes a huge amount of computing power to run VR games smoothly, so VR fans love being able to beef up their machines with the latest hardware.

Even with all this exciting new technology, sometimes the best thing about PC gaming is revisiting the classics. If you want to play your favorite old console games, you might need to hook up an old system and dig your cartridges out of a closet. Or, worse, you might have to pay high prices to buy these things because they have become collectibles. On a PC, you always have access to your old games. And even if those games don't work perfectly on modern hardware, you can be assured that someone out there is working on a mod or a patch to fix the problem. From the very beginning, PC gaming has been a hobby for people who love to tinker with their machines and maybe even create their own games. Some things never change!

For some PC gamers, the ability to enjoy the latest VR technology is a big part of the fun.

GLOSSARY

code (KOHD) instructions for a computer written using a programming language

developers (dih-VEL-uh-purz) people who make video games or other computer programs

esports (EE-sports) professional video game competitions

frame rate (FRAYM RAYT) a measurement of how many times per second the image on screen changes when playing a game

hardware (HARD-wair) the physical parts that make up a computer

mods (MAHDZ) user-created additions to video games

operating system (AH-pur-ay-ting SIS-tuhm) a program, such as Microsoft Windows or macOS, that controls the functions of a computer

patch (PATCH) an update to a game or other computer program that is created after the program is released

servers (SUR-vurz) computers that host files or perform services for other computers that connect through a network

upgraded (UP-gray-did) replaced something with a better version

FIND OUT MORE

Books

Cunningham, Kevin. *Video Game Designer*. Ann Arbor, MI: Cherry Lake Publishing, 2016.

Loh-Hagan, Virginia. *Video Games*. Ann Arbor, MI: Cherry Lake Publishing, 2021.

Powell, Marie. *Asking Questions About Video Games*. Ann Arbor, MI: Cherry Lake Publishing, 2016.

Websites

Logical Increments
www.logicalincrements.com/
This incredibly useful website will help you find parts that work well together and see how much they cost.

PC Gamer
www.pcgamer.com/
Keep up with the latest PC gaming news.

INDEX